It's often said that the pulpit driv[es] ... [over]looked is the role of gifted, godly t[eachers in] groups. The church needs not only [pastors to] point us to Jesus, but also teachers and leaders ... [filled] with love for Christ and love for the lost. *Gospel-Centered Teaching* will help accomplish this important goal. Superbly written, it is an accessible and helpful guide for leaders who want to ensure that their teaching of the written Word is always pointing others to the Living Word. This will be an extremely valuable tool for the building up of the body of Christ.

—Danny Akin, President of The Southeastern Baptist Theological Seminary, Wake Forest, NC

Pastors, if you are looking for a small book of great impact to give to all your teachers and group leaders this year, *Gospel-Centered Teaching* by Trevin Wax is it. Written to help teachers ground their task in Christ, this book points them to a big God and his sufficient Word, not easy shortcuts or new methods. You will love it and love how much it helps your teachers.

—Jason Duesing, Vice President for Strategic Initiatives and Assistant Professor of Historical Theology at The Southwestern Baptist Theological Seminary, Fort Worth, TX

A helpful resource steeped in good theology and imminently accessible. Perfect for those looking to teach practical insight in the context of the grand narrative.

—J.D. Greear, Pastor of Summit Church in Raleigh, NC and author of *Gospel: Recovering the Power That Made Christianity Revolutionary* and *Stop Asking Jesus Into Your Heart: How to Know For Sure You Are Saved*

Many of us teach the Bible using our instincts—instincts honed through years of Sunday school lessons and small group discussions that focused on how to follow the example of a biblical character or how to apply what we've read to our lives right now. To overcome these instincts we've got to become convinced there is a better way and provided with tools to retrain them. That's just what *Gospel-Centered Teaching* provides. Whether you've been teaching for years or are just getting started, you'll gain something from this accessible book. I sure did.

—Nancy Guthrie, author of the
***Seeing Jesus in the Old Testament Bible* study series**

Gospel-Centered Theology has fast become a popular term in American Christianity to call us back to the role of the power of Jesus in every area of life. Yet it also has become an unclear genre within American Christianity. In many ways it has become a movement, but in other ways it has become a fad. Hopefully in our generation, we will see the Lord use this movement in the grand scheme of people coming to know Jesus for the first time and believers understanding that we grow by that same gospel. That is why, Trevin's resource *Gospel-Centered Teaching* is a great aid to serve pastor's, teacher's, and disciple makers. Whenever there is a movement, there has to be resources that serve, resource, and focus it for long-term sustainability. Hopefully this resource will be used to do this in our time and beyond.

—Eric Mason, Lead Pastor of Epiphany
Fellowship, Philadelphia, PA and President of Thriving

Bible teachers or small group leaders often ask a lot of questions in order to grow in their craft. Trevin raises the question teachers should ask: How can one center every message on Jesus and what he has done? I'll be handing out this wonderful resource to many folks because Trevin explains the what, why, and how of Gospel-centered teaching so clearly and concisely.

—Tony Merida, Pastor of
Imago Dei Church, Raleigh, NC

At some point every preacher, teacher or small group leader will hear someone express disappointment with their teaching by suggesting that he or she want to "go deeper." While these disappointed Bible students may not really know what they mean by "going deeper," I suspect they may have a correct notion that something's missing from our teaching. If we begin a quest to find "what's" missing, we'll likely embark on an endless search for "new and better" methods and curricula. In *Gospel-Centered Teaching*, Trevin Wax wisely points us to the right question—"Who's missing?" The answer, of course, is Jesus. When we ask "Who's missing?" from our preaching/teaching, we'll embark on a quest to find Christ in all of Scripture. In this short, conversational, and extremely practical book, Trevin serves as an excellent guide who leads us to understand how to teach the Bible with Christ as our focus, the gospel as our center and the entire Bible as one big story about Jesus. If you want to teach a Christian lesson or preach a Christian sermon that glorifies our Savior and leads the church to live on mission, then you'll want to read this book!

—Juan R. Sanchez Jr., Preaching Pastor of
High Pointe Baptist Church, Austin, TX

Theologically robust teaching and missional passion don't have to be at odds with each other. Properly understood, solid teaching fuels mission because it leads us to Jesus Christ, the

Son of God who was sent and now sends. Trevin Wax has given us a brief, easy-to-understand guide to what it means to be focused on Christ in our teaching. I recommend pastors give the book to all their volunteer leaders and teachers. I know I will.

—Ed Stetzer, pastor of Grace Church and President of LifeWay Research, Nashville, TN

The apostle Paul writes in 1 Corinthians 4 that Jesus is the foundation of the church and we must take care how we build upon this foundation. As a pastor, I am primarily concerned with making sure that every gathering and every ministry of our church is rooted in the gospel of Jesus Christ. Since my calling is to equip the saints for the work of the ministry (Eph. 4:12), it is of critical importance that all the leaders of our church are trained to root all their teaching, counseling, and serving in the gospel. I am so thankful for this concise and very practical book, *Gospel-Centered Teaching*. I plan on distributing this to every one of our community group leaders and I highly recommend all pastors to get this book in the hands of their teachers and lay leaders.

—Afshin Ziafat, Lead Pastor of Providence Church, Frisco, TX

GOSPEL-
CENTERED
Teaching

TREVIN WAX

GOSPEL-CENTERED

Teaching

Showing Christ in All the Scripture

PUBLISHING GROUP
NASHVILLE, TENNESSEE

978-1-4336-8172-1

Published by B&H Publishing Group
Nashville, Tennessee

Dewey Decimal Classification: 220.07
Subject Heading: BIBLE—STUDY AND TEACHING \
GOSPEL \ TEACHING—RELIGIOUS ASPECTS

2 3 4 5 6 7 8 • 19 18 17 16 15

Dedication

For teachers and small group leaders who love Jesus,
love the church, and love the lost

Acknowledgments

Gospel-Centered Teaching is not just the title of a book, but also the affirmation of a Christ-focused approach to the Bible intended to lead God's people to join His mission to seek and save the lost. I'm grateful for the many pastors, preachers, and teachers in my life who never used the term "gospel-centered" but always turned my gaze to Christ. In the past few years, it's been a privilege to travel across the country and meet teachers and small group leaders who "do the work" of ministry every week without receiving fanfare or recognition. You open the Bible and open your group discussion, prayerfully guiding people to an encounter with

Christ again and again. I hope this book reignites your passion for leading and teaching.

I'm thankful for Bill Craig, Eric Geiger, Jennifer Lyell, and Devin Maddox for believing in the message of this book and encouraging me to develop a hands-on, practical guide to focusing our attention on Jesus. Thanks also to Ed Stetzer and Daniel Davis and all the team members, editors, and writers who make The Gospel Project a Christ-centered resource for people of all ages. Special thanks to my wife, Corina, who has cheered me on during the launch of The Gospel Project and throughout the writing of this book. Finally, I'm most grateful for the grace and mercy of Jesus Christ, who has saved me from my sin and sent me out at a witness to His gospel. May He get all the praise!

Contents

1

Something's Missing

 Can we have a heart-to-heart? You know, teacher to teacher? Maybe you steer clear of titles like "teacher" and instead think of yourself as a small group leader, or a "facilitator" of discussion with your group as you study the Scriptures. That's fine. Whatever title you use, the responsibility is the same: leading people to study the Bible and praying they see their lives transformed as a result.

Big responsibility, isn't it? And if you're honest, you'll probably admit that the task of teaching weighs on you from time to time. You know what an important role this is. You've heard the apostle James's warning (James 3:1) about teachers being held to a higher standard. Whether you're just starting out as a teacher or you've been in this role for decades, you know this is a big deal. People make choices based on what they understand in the Scriptures. Knowing God and His will is life or death. And you are stepping into a big role in helping people know how to read the Bible and understand what it means to live for Jesus.

If you're like me, you feel uneasy about all this sometimes. Your schedule is packed with things that fight for your attention. Spare time is hard to find, and even harder to find is the mental energy needed to study. It's difficult enough to maintain a daily rhythm of personal Bible reading, much less spend enough time in preparation to lead your group. That's why, some weeks, it feels like you're just going through the motions. Things seem to go all right, but you worry that you're not taking this stuff seriously enough.

I've been there. I've led small groups, taught traditional Sunday school, facilitated discussion (or whatever you call the "guided learning" type of model), and helped with home groups. I know the struggle. And nowadays, whenever I get the opportunity to travel to different cities and speak about teaching, curriculum, ministry philosophy, and big words like pedagogy, I get to talk with group leaders from all ages and different backgrounds. People like you; people like us. The best part of meeting so many people is that I get to listen. And interestingly enough, I hear a lot of the same things, over and over again. It's like a catchy chorus you can't get out of your head. No matter where I go, I hear a common refrain and a number of concerns. Something's missing from our small groups.

"My group isn't outward focused at all."

The first concern is what I call "missional apathy." The group leader wants to see God work in amazing ways and bring people into His kingdom. But the group itself seems to be turned inward. There's little desire to engage unbelievers. Little desire to make an impact outside the walls of the church. Little desire to get involved in serving others. So the leader says things like this: "I keep harping on what our group is supposed to be doing, but it's like banging my head against a wall. They know what the Bible says they should do, but they're just not interested." In other words, lots of Bible study, but no missionary zeal.

"My group doesn't know much about the Bible."

The second concern is biblical illiteracy. The group leader usually has a passion for understanding God's Word and explaining it to others, but the group itself doesn't seem to know the Bible well at all. "The people in my group have been in church for years, but they don't know some basic truths the Bible teaches. I get depressed when I see things on Facebook. It's like they don't see the world the way a Christian should. I want to challenge them to go deeper, but I don't know how. Plus, I'm afraid I'll lose them." In other words, lots of church activity, but little Bible knowledge and little distinctiveness from the world.

"Our discussions always seem so shallow."

The third concern is a dissatisfying Bible study experience. Usually, this complaint comes from the small group facilitator who leads discussion about a passage in the

Bible or a theological topic. "I don't know what I'm doing wrong. No one really seems to know how to interpret the Bible, so the discussion veers off in all directions, with everyone talking about what they think about the passage, but not what the passage actually says." In other words, lots of talking, but no resolution on what the Bible means and how it applies.

We Need More than Quick Solutions

These problems seem like they're disconnected, maybe even opposed to the others. And you can find any number of books and leaders offering a quick fix.

- *The group without any missionary fervor?* They've got too much Bible study going on. They just need to get out more! Bust up that group and get them in homes as missional communities.
- *The group struggling with Bible knowledge?* Reclaim the lecture-style of teaching and give it to them straight! Give them homework, ditch the

time of fellowship at the beginning, and focus on the content.

- ***The group with shallow discussion?*** Stop spending so much time trying to interpret the Bible passage. Instead, discuss how the pastor interpreted the passage for his latest sermon. Spend some more time in fellowship so you can get into each other's lives and get messy.

You get the idea. All sorts of solutions are offered, ways to fix these problems. Church leaders want to help, so they offer new techniques to jump start your group again, fire up your teaching, or ignite great discussion. Sometimes, the idea is to mimic whatever a growing megachurch is doing. Copy the method and then get on with it.

I'm not against trying new things and implementing new ideas. But I don't think there is a silver bullet to accomplishing discipleship through small groups. There are strengths and weaknesses to every method and model, every study environment, and every philosophy behind how we seek to capture people's hearts with the truth of

God's Word in the context of community. Even though I have my own opinions as to what methods are preferable, this book isn't about technique. Other books do a fine job laying out the options and making the case for doing life together in different ways. This book is about making sure we communicate the message of the gospel for your group, no matter what model you use.

Is It the Method or the Message?

I get the feeling that a lot of leaders are weary of running to the newest fad. Tired of trying to stir up enthusiasm for doing the same old thing. They realize it's not enough to give a face-lift to an old idea or to whip up excitement for the newest method. That's why, in this book, we're not going to focus on the structure of your group. I'm convinced that the method is not what matters most anyway; it's the message. Get the message right, and God will work through a variety of methods. But miss the message, and the best methods in the world won't bring about transformation.

When people share their concerns about the state of their groups, I usually ask some follow-up questions. And the more I drill down with leaders, the more I realize we have a message problem, and not a method problem. Most of the time, the leaders are looking for a new method. But their concerns are really about the message.

It's amazing to hear children's Sunday school teachers, some who've been teaching for more than twenty years, say things like, "Sometimes, I feel like all we're telling these kids to do is share their toys and obey Mom and Dad." In other words, kids' ministry is all about telling kids what to do. The goal is having a church full of nice kids.

Move up a few grades and student ministers worry that all they're doing is telling kids what not to do. You go from "obey Mommy and Daddy," to "don't drink, do drugs, or have sex." For twelve years, kids get all the "do's" of Christianity and then during middle school and high school, they get all the "don'ts." So youth workers will say things like, "We want more than this, right? We want their hearts, not just their behavior, don't we?"

Leaders of adult groups tire of being the perpetual cheerleader for life as it currently is. "I feel like we're rushing to pull things out of the Bible that just aren't there. Like we're more concerned about being practical than anything else." In other words, Bible study seems to be centered on whatever topic the group considers most needed.

So even if the initial concerns are explained in terms of methods, the real rub with leaders and teachers is about the message. Just what are we doing when we open the Bible? What's the point? What's the goal? How do I know if this is really working?

There's a sense of uneasiness in the growing realization that from childhood until adulthood, no matter what method is used, the main message we seem to be getting across is this: "Being a Christian is all about being a nice person and making the world a better place." And the reason many leaders are uncomfortable with the current state of things is because they should be. They know that the Bible says much more.

Let's Go Deeper?

So what do we do? Once we put aside the ongoing conversations about the method, we can start examining the message—what it is we're getting across. That's a good start. And almost everyone who starts analyzing our message realizes that we need to go "deeper." The problem is, no one seems to agree on what "going deeper" looks like.

I once met a youth pastor who was so frustrated with accusations of "shallowness" and demands for "more depth" that he told me, "Fine! If they want to go deeper, I'm going to go so deep it drives them nuts. I'll drown them in depth!" Not exactly the best posture to take as a disciple-maker of the next generation.

I didn't like the youth pastor's attitude. But I did understand his frustration. Why? Because sometimes it's hard to please the people clamoring for "deeper" teaching when everyone seems to have a different idea of what "deep" is. That's why some leaders and teachers will change the subject and start talking about the methods again, because the "deeper" conversation about the message makes everyone want to throw their hands up in despair.

It's tricky trying to define "depth," but we're going to take a stab at it. To do so, we need to look at two common ways that people talk about "depth." Both are insufficient.

Depth as "Information"

A lot of folks think that their small group experience is "deep" if they learn something they didn't know beforehand. In other words, they want to close their Bibles at the end of group time with more information than they had when they opened them. *Give me more knowledge! Tell me something I didn't know!*

It really doesn't matter what the information is, as long as it's new, interesting, and makes everyone feel smarter. It can be information about an obscure archeological dig somewhere in the Middle East. Or it can be the careful parsing of the tense of a Greek verb. Whatever. The goal is "more knowledge."

Now, I've got to admit I sympathize with Christians who want more facts. When I was a missionary in Romania, I quickly realized just how blessed we are as English speakers. We have more resources available to us in our native tongue than ever before. It is astounding to consider all the information we have at our fingertips. (And the digital revolution has only increased our access to Bible study tools.)

But even with all these resources, people seem to know less and less about the Bible. Almost everyone agrees that we have a biblical illiteracy problem in the United States. It's an epidemic—even among people who have grown up in church. No one seems to be immune. A lot of the people in our groups have disjointed stories from the Bible floating around in their minds, but no one is quite sure how they all fit together. Even basic facts get mangled in our churches. When church members think Sodom and Gomorrah were a married couple, well, "Houston, we have a problem!"

Once you begin to think "depth" means "more knowledge," you are on track to produce an elitist class of people who view the Bible as their hobby. It was the ancient Gnostics who were all about "secret knowledge," not the Christians. The proper understanding of biblical knowledge and information is that it is a means to a greater end. The reason we study God's Word is because it tells us about God. We want to know more about God in order that we might know God more. The last thing we want is a closed-off group of biblical junkies who view Bible study as their "fix" for the week. Information alone is not the goal, and information is not depth.

So, rightly understood, the pursuit of knowledge is grounded in our desire to know and love God. But if we're not careful, the pursuit of knowledge is merely a sham to make ourselves feel intellectually superior to those around us. We start to view spiritual maturity in terms of knowledge rather than obedience. At the end of the day, we've got people who can win a game of Bible trivia, but who don't look very much like Jesus.

Theology matters, and we never need apologize for giving people information as we study the Bible. But surely we want to go deeper than the demons. They've got their theology down (James 2), but are devils still.

Depth as "Application"

On the other side of the spectrum are folks who think "deep" means "practical." They aren't so interested in gaining more knowledge; they just want to be told what to do. After all, the real need is for Christians to start applying what they already know to be true. "Information isn't the goal, transformation is!" says this group.

How does this play out? The leader who sees "going deep" as "applying the Scriptures" will make sure their group walks away with a number of practical ways to obey the Bible in their daily lives. The idea is to connect the Bible to the choices we make every day. Let's show people how the Bible affects what we're doing at school, at home, or in the workplace. Whatever passage you're studying, just make sure you launch into some practical tidbits for daily living.

Anyone can see why "life transformation" has such strong appeal. Surely we don't want people looking in the mirror of God's Word and then walking away, unaware of their reflection. Every teacher should hope for transformation. That's one of the main reasons you felt called to lead others in Bible study in the first place, right? God used someone in your life to help you see how the Scriptures apply to your life. You saw the relevance of following Jesus, and now you want to see others transformed by personal, practical application of God's Word.

But even though we're right to seek to apply the Bible to everyday life, we need to be careful not to reduce the Bible to a list of "do's and don'ts" for the week. The goal of Bible study isn't to send a group out into the world with an action plan every week. Why not? Because the Bible isn't first and foremost about us. It's God's message to us, yes. But it's ultimately about God. If all we draw from Bible study are proverb-like teachings for daily living, then we are approaching the Scriptures as if we're at the center.

Don't misunderstand me. The Bible has plenty to say about our daily lives. One of the truths we'll explore in this book is how gospel-grounded application speaks to all of life. So the impulse to connect the Bible to life is a good one. The problem is, if we jump too quickly to application in our teaching, over time we create self-absorbed readers who skim the Scriptures in search of personal application rather than the primary meaning of the text. We start seeing the Bible as if it were a self-help book, designed to enhance our current way of living.

In reality, God wants to explode our current way of living and offer us new life altogether. The Bible isn't an assistant to your old way of life. It's the doorway to your new life in Christ. Likewise, the story line of Scripture contains earth-shattering truths that can't be spiritualized into coffee-mug verses that give us warm fuzzes. Depth as application isn't enough.

The Depth of the Gospel

So if the answer isn't information or application, what is it? What's missing? Actually, the right question isn't "What's missing?" but "Who's missing?" Here's a question we should ponder: Where is Jesus in your Bible study? What role does the Spirit play in your preparation? How does the plan of redemption dreamed up in the heart of God the Father affect the way you read the Bible?

You see, we sometimes get so busy thinking that people need more information or better application that we forget that our main task is to lead people to exultation. That's a fancy word for "worship." We exult—we delight in the Savior we exalt. Exaltation of the Savior leads to exultation of the saints. The Bible is ultimately about Jesus, which means that Bible study ought to lead us to worship Him.

So what's this book about? Not a new technique. Not a new formula for success. In fact, there's hardly anything new in this book. No, my goal is to remind you of something you already instinctively know as a teacher of God's Word or a leader of a small group. It's Jesus who changes lives, and the goal of your Bible study is to continually reintroduce people to Him.

Should we give people information? Yes. Should we give people application? Yes. But most importantly, we must give people the gospel message because it transcends information and application, yet includes them both. My goal is to offer you a practical guide to making sure your message is centered on Jesus and what He has done. So let's get started!

2

Back to Basics

"Bible study won't necessarily change your life."

Just because you know the Bible doesn't mean the Word will bear fruit in your life. It is possible to know the Scriptures, read the Scriptures, revere the Scriptures, and study the Scriptures and miss the point entirely.

Take the academic scholar who knows the Greek New Testament better than most pastors. He can quote whole sections of the Bible in its original languages. Definitions of biblical words tumble out of his mouth as he effortlessly places biblical narrative in historical context. And yet many biblical scholars in the Academy do not believe in the Jesus of the Bible. They are endlessly fascinated by the communities that gave us such an interesting artifact of study, but that is all the Bible is to them—an ancient artifact. The unbelieving scholar immerses himself into a world of fables and dreams. To him, the Bible is just a fairy tale with no bearing on reality today.

Or take the Jewish leaders of Jesus' day, men who were steeped in the rich tradition of their people's history. These leaders knew the Scriptures backward and forward, but Jesus said they had missed the signs pointing to the most important chapter in the Story that God was writing—the chapter that had been foreshadowed by the prophets and Bible writers for thousands of years. That's why Jesus could say, "You pour over the Scriptures because you think you have eternal life in them, yet they testify about Me. And you are not willing to come to Me so that you may have life" (John 5:39–40). He didn't condemn them for their meticulous knowledge of the Old Testament. He mourned the fact that they'd missed the point of it all.

Even today, it's possible to get so wrapped up in searching the Scriptures that we miss what God is trying to teach us. Consider would-be prophets who scour over the prophecies of Revelation trying to pull out clues and codes about the European Union or the next major ecological catastrophe. Caught up in the thrill, the writers lose sight of Revelation's main purpose: to unveil Jesus!

Others get bogged down in theological discussions that cause them to read the Scriptures looking for more ammunition for their next debate. Meanwhile, the Bible quietly gets twisted into a divine reference book designed to uphold a beloved system of theology instead of God's divine revelation designed to shine light on a glorious Savior.

And then there's the type of Bible study we mentioned earlier, where we read the Bible as if we are at the center and need to bring God into our world to address our already-defined needs and problems. We look at the Bible as a book of divine instruction, a manual for succeeding in life, or a map for making sure we get to heaven when we die.

These ways of studying the Scripture will not ultimately result in life transformation, because they miss the point. The point is Jesus. That's why we can say that Bible study alone is not what transforms your life. Jesus transforms your life.

Of course, He does this through His written Word to us. So we mustn't think that life change takes place apart from God's Word. At the same time, we must recognize that the reason God's Word changes our life is not because of our personal study but because in the Scriptures we are introduced to Jesus, the Author. That's why every page ought to be written in red, as every section is breathed out by our King and points us to Him.

It's possible to amass great amounts of biblical knowledge, to impress people with your mastery of Bible trivia, to creatively apply the Bible in ways that seem so down-to-earth and practical, to dot your theological i's and cross your exegetical t's—and still miss Jesus. Scary, isn't it?

At the end of the day, it's not enough to be "Bible-believing" or "Word-centered," because, after all, the Bible we believe and the Word we proclaim is itself Christ-centered. I love the way one of the Baptist leaders of the previous generation described the Bible:

The Bible has one central theme: God's redemptive purpose. It has one central figure: Christ. It has one central goal: God supreme in a redeemed universe.

The Old Testament sounds the messianic hope. The Gospels record Christ's incarnation. Acts relates His continuing work through the Holy Spirit. The Epistles interpret His person and work. Revelation proclaims His final triumph and glory.

The Bible points forward to Christ, backward to Christ, and again forward to Christ in His glorious return and reign.

Forward, backward, and forward. Everywhere you turn, there is Christ.[1]

The purpose of our Bible study is to know God and make Him known. The Bible unveils Jesus Christ as the focal point of human history. All creation exists by Him, through Him, to Him, and for Him. Our Bible study should exist for Him too. That's the only kind of Bible study that will change your life.

Jesus Is the Answer

In the previous chapter, we saw how "going deep" can't be reduced to giving more information or better application. Instead, we must pursue the kind of depth that grounds us in the richness of the gospel. If we are to be gospel-centered teachers and leaders, then we must be ever focused on the person and work of King Jesus. After all, the gospel is about Him.

There's a running joke in evangelical circles that has to do with the questions we ask kids in Sunday school. What's the answer to every Sunday school question? "Jesus." To do it right and get the laugh, you have to mimic your best preschooler voice and leave it open-ended, as if you really aren't sure: "Jeeesus?" Even in adult small groups, whenever the leader throws out a question that others don't know the answer to, some smart aleck will break the tension by giving "Jesus" as the answer.

This is one way that evangelicals poke fun at some of the simplistic "Sunday school" answers that are common in church. But putting the humor aside for a moment, I want to point out the profundity of that answer. Yes, we kid around about the easy questions we ask preschoolers, but at the end of the day, what is better than leading the smallest children to know Jesus is the answer? In a very real sense, the answer to all of life's biggest problems is summed up in Jesus. It's no joke.

Why Gospel-Centered?

I bet some of you are on board with me now and are ready to get into the nitty-gritty details of how to be more Christ-focused and gospel-centered in your teaching. You're ready to see what this looks like in practice. Hang with me. In the next chapter, we're going to get into the specifics of how to ensure that Christ is front and center in our Bible study. But first, we need to do a little more explaining about why our teaching should take us back to the basics, back to the gospel. If you jump to the practical stuff and miss the "why," you'll be tempted to try something else when the going gets tough. You'll be inclined to put your trust in the power of something other than the gospel to bring about life change.

There are probably others who are reading this who still have an eyebrow raised. You hear about this "gospel-centered" language and aren't sure what all the fuss is about. You may be asking why this is necessary. That's why I'd like to offer a few reasons why we're having this conversation in the first place, why being gospel-centered really does matter.

1. Because the Gospel Is the Power of God unto Salvation

The first reason we need to be centered on the gospel as we lead others to study God's Word is because the gospel is powerful. It's the good news of Jesus Christ that saves sinners. The apostle Paul described the gospel as "God's power for salvation" (Rom. 1:16).

At one level, this truth is constraining. It ought to chain us to the biblical text. At another level, it is freeing. It reminds us that the power to save is not in our expert teaching skills, but in the power of God's Spirit working through God's Word.

Just think about the strangeness of the gospel message for a moment. We live in the twenty-first century, a time of technological wonders. We can travel across the ocean in the air. We can accomplish more on a single cell phone than scientists fifty years ago could accomplish through computers that filled entire warehouses. Advances in medical technology and sanitation have led to the diminishment of all sorts of illnesses and diseases. Scientists marvel at the complexity of DNA as they seek to unravel the mysteries of the universe.

We live in a scientific age of technological revolution. Yet, today we call people to believe that two thousand years ago, a messiah figure from a backwater town in an obscure part of the Roman Empire was crucified as an imposter and then walked out of His grave the next Sunday morning. Not only that, this messiah is the true King of the world, and even though you cannot see Him, He demands nothing less than total allegiance from you and everyone else on the planet, regardless of social status, religious affiliation, race, ethnicity, or nationality.

What is intuitive about this message? Is there anything in this message that would make you say, "Oh, that makes perfect sense! Everyone is naturally going to believe that." Nope. No wonder the skeptics scoff and the comedians mock. Think about how strange the gospel is to the natural mind.

It's not just scientific advancements that make the gospel seem strange. In the days of the early church, the apostle Paul saw the image of a crucified messiah to be a stumbling block to the Jews and to the Gentiles. There was something to offend everyone. And yet, for two millennia, against all odds, people have found themselves convinced of this message, and in response to the Holy Spirit's conviction of sin have chosen to reorient their entire lives around this Savior and King in whom they put their trust.

People just keep on believing the gospel. Why? Because the gospel is such an easy message to believe? No. Because the gospel is powerful. The Spirit works powerfully through the gospel to bring us to salvation.

I ask you, leader to leader: Do you sense your neediness? Are you aware of your dependence on the Spirit of God to break the hearts of lost people and woo them to the beloved Savior who died for them? The last thing we need is another formula guaranteed to make our group grow or a flashy teaching method that will keep everyone entertained. What we need most is to fall on our knees before an almighty God and beg Him to work through us. Apart from Him, we can do nothing.

Until we understand that the gospel is the power of God for salvation, we will never reach that moment of holy desperation on the Spirit of God. Unless you understand the power of life transformation is in the gospel, you'll run after anything and everything else trying to manufacture life change.

Not too long ago, I was discouraged. I had been engaged in some spiritual conversations with some friends who don't know Jesus. After weeks of praying for them and sharing Christ with them, I began to realize these friends were farther away from Christ than I had thought. Our conversations seemed to be going well at first, but later discussions had revealed to me just how entrenched they were in their views opposing Christianity.

Discouraged and disappointed, I remember thinking to myself, *It's going to take a miracle for my friends to get saved.* And in that moment, the Spirit reminded me: It always does. Of course, it will take a miracle! Every conversion is a supernatural work, a miraculous occurrence when a sinner repents and believes and receives a heart of flesh in place of a heart of stone. I don't know what had gotten into me. Had I seriously thought that it would be my persuasive charm that would bring about their conversion? That the power of salvation would be found in the way I packaged and presented the gospel? The dynamite isn't the packaging, but what's inside—the glorious gospel of Jesus Christ that has been melting hearts and defying expectations for two thousand years now. We need to be gospel-centered because that's where the power is. It's not in me. It's not in you. It's in God.

2. Because the Gospel Is the Power of God for Sanctification

A second reason we should be gospel-centered is because the gospel is the power of God for our sanctification. It's the message God uses to grow us in holiness and conform us to the image of His Son.

Too many times, we assume that the gospel is just the basics of the Christian life, but that intense, deep discipleship takes place when we get into the theological precision of interpreting biblical doctrines. Sometimes, we can unintentionally communicate such a thing by the way we separate new believers from "mature" believers. As if the gospel is only for the newbies, while the rest of us can go on to the deeper stuff.

Not so. The gospel is the message that gives richness and profundity to all our study of the Bible. It's often said that John 3:16 is simple enough for a child to believe, and yet we can linger over these words for a lifetime and never exhaust all the truth contained here.

We never "get over" the gospel. We never "move beyond" the gospel. Why in the world would we even try to "move beyond" the beautiful truth that God loved the world by giving His Son that we could have eternal life with Him? Think of your heart, your sins, your past, and your failures. Think of your wretched state of wickedness and your rebellion against your Creator. And now consider the magnificence of God's love in that He would willingly give His Son to redeem you and bring you into His family. What kind of love seeks out rebels and welcomes them to His table?

In 1 Corinthians 15:2, Paul spoke of the gospel as the message "by which you are being saved." The gospel isn't just what saves us, but it's also what sustains us. We hold fast to the God who is holding fast to us.

Bible study involves more than training people to win a game of Bible trivia. It's more than finding immediate application for our lives tomorrow. If the only thing we have when we leave a time of Bible study is more head knowledge and a spiritual to-do list for the week, we've missed the point. We need our hearts to be wrecked afresh by the reality of God's love for us. We need Jesus.

We progress in holiness the more we immerse ourselves in the truth that Jesus Christ bled and died to save helpless sinners like you and me. The more we see the depth of our sin, the more we understand the depth of God's grace. Going deep means we must remember there is nothing we can do to make ourselves more acceptable to God.

The gospel-centered teacher understands that the unsaved need the gospel in order to come to know Christ, while the saved need the gospel in order to become more like Christ. That's why at the heart of this message is the costly grace we sing about, the grace that demands "my life, my soul, my all."[2]

It's been said that the gospel is not just the ABCs of salvation, but the A to Z of the Christian life. We never move beyond this good news. As we study the Scriptures, we begin to better understand the truth of the gospel and all its implications.

3. Because the Gospel Provides the Motivation for Mission

"Why aren't our small groups or Sunday school classes making an impact outside the church walls?" you may say to yourself. Now, we're back to one of the common concerns leaders have about their groups: missional apathy. And this brings us to the third reason why we need to be gospel-centered. The Spirit of God uses the gospel of God to motivate the people of God to be on mission with God.

Too often, when we recognize that our church needs to refocus on mission, we turn to solutions that depend on outward activities and not inward realities. We need a paradigm shift. When we notice our small groups are not engaged in the mission of God, we should look beyond the symptoms to the root cause.

We need to ask tough questions: Why aren't people excited to fulfill the Great Commission? What is causing apathy when it comes to proclaiming the gospel?

These questions push us back into gospel territory. What exactly is the gospel? What does the gospel have to do with life today, not just life after death? What is the gospel's purpose for a Christian once we've been saved?

You see, the root cause of our lack of engagement in God's mission is not a missions problem but a gospel problem. We demonstrate by our inaction that we no longer marvel at grace. We are unaffected by the beauty of what God has done for us in Christ.

As leaders, we want to introduce people to Jesus. We want to see people's hearts overflowing with love for Jesus and love for others. In fact, if you recall your early passion for teaching, that's probably the reason you got into this whole business in the first place. You loved Jesus and wanted others to know Him too. And nothing will motivate you and your group to be on mission for God's kingdom more than knowing and loving the King of kings.

What Is the Gospel?

Before we jump into the practical ways of being gospel-centered in our teaching, it's important to get on the same page when it comes to the gospel itself. So, please bear with me as we finish laying the foundation before launching into the practical stuff.

It's always interesting to poll long-time Christians to hear how they respond to the question "what is the gospel?" The variety of responses among church leaders is always interesting to note. People hear this question in different ways, and then they answer accordingly.

Salvation for an Individual

Some immediately think of the gospel in terms of presenting the message to an individual. It's the Romans Road approach that starts with a holy God who created the world and human beings made in His image who have rebelled against Him and are deserving of death. But thanks be to God for sending His Son Jesus to die on the cross for our sins and rise from the dead to give us new life! The presentation ends with a call to repent of sin and believe in Christ. More recently, this approach has been summarized under four headings: God, Man, Christ, Response.

The Story of Jesus

Others hear the question "what is the gospel?" and think exegetically. In other words, they think about what the word *gospel* means in the New Testament. Take this approach and you'll wind up focusing squarely on Jesus Christ and what He has done. Generally, the announcement of Jesus is going to take into consideration His perfect life, His substitutionary death, His resurrection, and His exaltation. Evangelism happens when you walk with a lost person through one of the Gospels. This group looks for how the word *gospel* is used in the New Testament, and they define the word accordingly.

The Narrative of New Creation

Then there's the group that sees the "gospel" as the coming kingdom of God. It's the whole good news of Christianity written from the beginning of creation to the establishment of new creation and the consummation of all things when Jesus returns. Evangelism with this group is going to focus on the need to join the gospel community (the church) and become a foretaste of the coming king-dom. God saves us through the death and resurrection of His Son and then recruits us for His ongoing work of redeeming the lost and restoring the world.

Defining the "Gospel"

Whenever I'm in a group setting with church lead-ers and I present these three ways of hearing the "what is the gospel?" question, I poll everyone there and ask them which answer they naturally gravitate toward. Almost always, they're divided evenly.

I don't think we need to pit these gospel definitions against the others. All of them have biblical precedent. The first recognizes the need to provide a compelling, simple presentation for an unbeliever. The second recog-nizes the need to stay biblical in how we use words and to focus attention on Jesus. The third recognizes the need for the gospel to be understood within the biblical story line and the worldview that story provides. Truth be told, we don't need just one of these approaches; we need them all.

So, when it comes down to it, here's how we might put these things together. We begin with the gospel proper, the announcement of Jesus Christ. Then, we move to the gospel's context (the story line of the Bible), and finally to the gospel's purpose (creating the church).

The Gospel Proper (The Announcement)

The gospel is the royal announcement that Jesus Christ, the Son of God, lived a perfect life in our place, died a substitutionary death on the cross for our sins, rose triumphantly from the grave to launch God's new creation, and is now exalted as King of the world. This announcement calls for a response: repentance (mourning over and turning from our sin, trading our agendas for the kingdom agenda of Jesus Christ) and faith (trusting in Christ alone for salvation).

The Gospel's Context (The Story of Scripture)

The Bible tells us about God's creation of a good world which was subjected to futility because of human sin. God chose the people of Israel and gave them the Law to reveal His holiness and our need for a perfect sacrifice, which is provided by the death of the Messiah—Jesus Christ. This same Jesus will one day return to this earth to judge the living and the dead and thus renew all things. The gospel story is the scriptural narrative that takes us from creation to new creation, climaxing with the death and resurrection of Jesus at the center.

The Gospel's Purpose (The Community)

The gospel births the church. We are shaped by the gospel into the kind of people who herald the grace of God and spread the news of Jesus Christ. God has commissioned the church to be the community that embodies the message of the gospel. Through our corporate life together, we "obey the gospel" by living according to the truth of the message that Jesus Christ is Savior and Lord of the world.

Centered on the Gospel

So how do we do this well? How do we point others to Jesus? How do we get back to the gospel?

Sometimes teachers and preachers decide that the way to be gospel-centered is to tack on a gospel presentation to the end of a message, a sermon, or a time of discussion. Presenting the gospel this way is good. It's certainly better than having a gospel-less message altogether.

But if we're not careful, by tacking on a bullet point presentation to the end of our talks, we can communicate that the gospel doesn't have much to do with everything else we've been talking about. In other words, if the gospel seems disjointed from the rest of your sermon or the rest of your small group experience, you probably need to go back to the drawing board.

You want the truths of the gospel to impact the way you do everything—from theology, to application, to any subject you're discussing. The way you help your people understand that the gospel is for all of life is not by telling them the gospel pervades everything, but by showing them in how you teach.

The gospel isn't the dessert at the end of the meal. It's the salt that gives distinctive flavor to the meat and potatoes. The gospel is what makes our teaching distinctively Christian. And Jesus is at the heart of the gospel. If we don't get back to Him, we miss out on the power of the Christian life.

In order to be gospel-centered, I suggest you ask three major questions of every lesson you prepare, sermon you preach, or discussion time you facilitate. No matter what passage of Scripture you're studying, what practical topic you're discussing, or theological truth you are presenting, you ought to ask these three questions:

1. How does this topic/passage fit into the big story of Scripture?
2. What is distinctively Christian about the way I am addressing the topic/passage? (Would this be true if Jesus hadn't died and been raised?)

3. How does this truth equip God's church to live on mission?

These questions are a helpful guide to keeping Christ as the focus of our ministry. In the next three chapters, I'd like to show you why.

3

Connect the Dots
and Tell the Story

 One of the questions you ought to ask of every lesson you prepare is this: "How does this topic or passage fit into the big story of Scripture?" Why is this question important? Because it reminds you to show your group how the Bible fits together.

Not long ago, I was talking to a young man who was reading through the Bible for the first time. I gave him the broad outline of the Bible's story line and told him how the individual stories were pointing forward to the big story of Jesus Christ. He admitted he had little knowledge of the Scriptures, but he wanted to know where Noah's Ark fits into it all. Apparently, he remembered the story of Noah, perhaps from having heard it as a child. But that was all he knew. As he read through his Bible, he saw the stories in much the same way people read Aesop's Fables—short, memorable tales with a moral at the end.

I can't fault an unchurched, lost man for not reading the Bible as one overarching story. After all, he's not a Christian. No one has told him how these stories point to Jesus.

Unfortunately, I have found that plenty of people in church are not much better at interpreting the Scriptures. Granted, we usually know a higher number of Bible stories. Churchgoers know more than just the story of Noah. Names like Daniel, David, Moses, and Solomon are familiar. But for many of us, we see the purpose of these stories to inculcate moral values. From David, we learn about courage. From Daniel, we learn about determination. From Abraham, we learn about faith. From Solomon, we learn about wisdom. And on and on.

To be fair, we need to recognize that the Old Testament heroes are indeed presented as an example for us. The apostle Paul said so (1 Cor. 10). We can and should learn about persistence from Noah, courage from David, determination from Daniel, and endurance from Moses. To minimize the moral teaching in the Old Testament and never explore how these characters should be emulated is to misread the Bible at a profound level. So, on the one hand, we are exactly right to understand that one of the reasons we are given the Old Testament stories is so that we might be formed into more virtuous believers.

But the Bible doesn't just present heroes to be followed. After all, these heroes are flawed. We admire Noah for his tenacity in building an ark while his neighbors mocked his plans. What a portrait of faith, right? But after the flood, we see Noah in a drunken stupor, naked in his tent. Not the way we usually end the story when we're telling it to our kids, is it?

We love watching David slay the giant and cut off his head. The shepherd boy, described as "a man after God's own heart." But then he lusts after a woman, commits adultery, schemes to cover it up, and has her husband killed. Think about it. Many of the psalms we sing in church were written by a philandering murderer!

So what to do? The heroes of the Old Testament are there for us to learn from—both good traits to be cultivated and bad traits to be avoided. But these heroes serve another purpose. Their stories point us toward the flawless One. They are heroes, but only in a secondary sense. God is the true Hero of the Bible, and we see the most heroic action of all in the rescue mission accomplished by His Son. If you teach the Bible as if it is a collection of stand-alone tales, your people will never see how these stories connect to tell the big story of salvation through Jesus Christ.

The Story of the Bible

What is the story of the Bible? Most scholars divide the story line into four movements: Creation, Fall, Redemption, and Restoration. These four headings serve as a helpful reminder of how the Bible fits together.

When we were starting work on The Gospel Project,[3] we decided to summarize the whole Bible in three hundred words. We wanted to trace the biblical story line in a way that incorporated these four elements and ended with a call to respond with repentance and faith.

Here is how we summarized the Bible's grand narrative:

In the beginning, the all-powerful, personal God created the universe. This God created human beings in His image to live joyfully in His presence, in humble submission to His gracious authority. But all of us have rebelled against God and, in consequence, must suffer the punishment of our rebellion: physical death and the wrath of God.

Thankfully, God initiated a rescue plan, which began with His choosing the nation of Israel to display His glory in a fallen world. The Bible describes how God acted mightily on Israel's behalf, rescuing His people from slavery and then giving them His holy law. But God's people—like all of us—failed to rightly reflect the glory of God.

Then, in the fullness of time, in the Person of Jesus Christ, God Himself came to renew the world and restore His people. Jesus perfectly obeyed the law given to Israel. Though innocent, He suffered the consequences of human rebellion by His death on a cross. But three days later, God raised Him from the dead.

Now the church of Jesus Christ has been commissioned by God to take the news of Christ's work to the world. Empowered by God's Spirit, the church calls all people everywhere to repent of sin and to trust in Christ alone for our forgiveness. Repentance and faith restores our relationship with God and results in a life of ongoing transformation.

The Bible promises that Jesus Christ will return to this earth as the conquering King. Only those who live in repentant faith in Christ will escape God's judgment and live joyfully in God's presence for all eternity. God's message is the same to all of us: repent and believe, before it is too late. Confess with your mouth that Jesus is Lord and believe in your heart that God raised Him from the dead, and you will be saved.

Why Do We Need the Bible's Story Line?

Some of you may be wondering why so many people are talking about the Bible's story line lately. What's the big deal? Why is it so important for Christians to be able to connect the dots of the Bible's grand narrative? Here are four reasons.

1. To Gain a Biblical Worldview

The first reason we need to keep the biblical story line in mind is because the narrative of the Bible is the narrative of the world. The Bible doesn't just give us commands and prohibitions. It gives us an entire worldview.

We all live according to a worldview. A worldview is the lens through which we see the world and make decisions. It's like wearing a pair of glasses. You don't think about looking at your glasses when you have them on. You look through them to see the world around you. Everyone has a worldview, even people who are not Christians.

Unfortunately, there are many Christians who do not have a Christian worldview. They may display some of the religious trappings of Christianity, but they demonstrate by their choices that they are living by another worldview.

The story line of the Bible is important because it helps us think as Christians formed by the great Story that tells the truth about our world. It is vitally important that people know the overarching story line of the Bible that leads from creation, to our fall into sin, to redemption through Jesus Christ, and final restoration in the fullness of time. If we are to live as Christians in a fallen world, we must be shaped by the grand narrative of the Scriptures, the worldview we find in the Bible.

2. To Recognize and Reject False Worldviews

A few years ago, two sociologists studying the religious views of young people in North America coined the phrase "moralistic therapeutic deism."[4] Those are three big words that sum up the following five beliefs of many in our society today:

1. "A god exists who created and ordered the world and watches over human life on earth." (That's the "Deism" part. God created the world, watches things, but doesn't do much in the way of intervening in human affairs.)

2. "God wants people to be good, nice, and fair to each other, as taught in the Bible and by most world religions." (That's the Moralistic part. The goal of religion is to be a nice, moral person.)

3. "The central goal of life is to be happy and to feel good about oneself." (That's the Therapeutic part. The most important thing in life is to be happy and well-balanced.)

4. "God does not need to be particularly involved in one's life except when God is needed to resolve a problem." (Now, we see the Deistic view of God combine with God's therapeutic purpose. He exists to make us happy.)

5. "Good people go to heaven when they die." (Salvation is accomplished through morality.)

Moralistic Therapeutic Deism. "Moralism," for short. Our society is awash in this worldview. Even longtime church members are not immune to it.

So, if we are going to be effective witnesses to the gospel in our day and age, we must put forth a biblical view of the world that counters rival worldviews. Just think, if you were called to be a missionary to India, wouldn't you first study Hinduism to see how it affects the culture and the people's view of God there? Wouldn't part of your strategy be to show how Christianity counters the Hindu worldview? Likewise, if you were called to be a missionary to Iran, would you not study the worldview of Muslims and see where Christianity and Islam diverge? A good missionary knows what Christianity teaches as opposed to what the dominant worldview of the culture says, even if that worldview is the moralistic therapeutic deism of the United States.

3. To Rightly Understand the Gospel

Another reason we need to know the story line of the Bible is because the gospel can quickly become distorted without it. The story of the Bible gives context to the gospel message about Jesus.

Too many times, we think of the gospel as a story that jumps from the garden of Eden (we've all sinned) right to the cross (but Jesus fixes everything). On its own, that works fine in communicating the systematic points of our need for salvation and God's provision in Christ, but from a biblical and theological perspective, it doesn't do justice to what's actually in the text. Once a person becomes a Christian and cracks the Bible, they're going to wonder what the big deal is about Israel and the covenant, since that storyline takes up roughly seventy-five percent of the Bible. Getting people into that story is important. As D. A. Carson says, the announcement is incoherent without it.[5]

I once spent significant time witnessing to a coworker, one of those "all religions lead to God-consciousness" sorts of guys. He and I went back and forth on the gospel. Eventually, he admitted that he believed Jesus had been bodily raised from the dead. Yet his explanation of the resurrection was this: God raised Jesus from the dead because He'd been unjustly condemned, and His purpose in rising was to demonstrate His God-consciousness so He could beckon us to learn from Him. In other words, Jesus was still just Master Teacher and not Savior and Lord. My coworker got the bare facts of the announcement right, and yet the story he was working from was wrong. The story line affected the announcement to the point where he really didn't believe the gospel at all.

We need the biblical story line in order to understand the gospel of Jesus. Otherwise, sharing the gospel of Christ's death and resurrection is like coming into a movie theater at the most climactic moment but without any knowledge of the story thus far. You will be able to discern bits and pieces of the story, but you won't understand the full significance of what is happening unless you know the backstory.

4. To Keep Our Focus on Christ

There has been a lot of talk in recent years about making the gospel announcement of Jesus Christ front and center in our preaching and teaching. As our society becomes increasingly post-Christian, it is critical for us to not assume lost people know who God is, what He is like, and what He has done for us. We need to be clear in what we teach, with a laser-like focus on Jesus Christ our Savior. The biblical story line helps us do this.

Every story has a main character. The Bible does too. It's God. Specifically, it's God as He reveals Himself to us in the Person of Jesus Christ.

Here's what happens if we learn individual Bible stories and never connect them to the big Story. We put ourselves in the scene as if we are the main character. We take the moral examples of the Old and New Testament as if they were there to help us along in the life we've chosen for ourselves.

But the more we read the Bible, the more we see that God is the main character, not us. We are not the heroes learning to overcome all obstacles, persist in our faith, and call down fire from heaven. We're the ones who need rescue, who need a Savior who will deliver us from Satan, sin, and death. It's only in bowing before the real Hero of the story that we are in the right posture to take our place in the unfolding drama. Bearing in mind the big story of Scripture helps us keep our focus on Jesus, and off ourselves.

How Do We Connect the Dots?

So now you're thinking, *This all sounds great, but how do I make sure that Jesus is center stage in our church? How do we keep other things from taking His place in our sermons, our Sunday school classes or our small groups? How do I point people back to the big story of the Bible that has Christ as the Hero?*

I mentioned earlier that the "big story" question ("How does this topic or passage fit into the big picture story of the Bible?") will help you as a pastor or teacher to connect the dots for your people. We need to help people learn to read the Bible for themselves, to understand the flow of the narrative, how the different genres fit into that narrative, and how to wisely apply the truths of the Bible. Here are several suggestions:

1. Read through the Bible chronologically.

You're not going to be able to connect the dots for the people you lead if you do not understand the story line of the Bible. You've got to be aware, not only of the big headings (Creation, Fall, Redemption, Restoration), but also the order in which different themes move through the Bible.

One of the best ways to see the grand narrative of Scripture is to read through the Bible chronologically. There are a number of Bibles in English that provide a chronological reading plan. I suggest using *Read the Bible for Life* by George Guthrie.

First, check out the book itself. *Read the Bible for Life* contains interviews with scholars who offer principles that help you interpret the Bible's various styles of literature.

Next, check out the *Read the Bible for Life* chronological reading plan. It includes brief commentary on each day's reading. Nothing will help you understand the grand narrative of Scripture more than reading the Scriptures yourself.

2. Read at least one Bible overview book a year.

I also suggest reading at least one "Bible overview" book a year. Here are some suggestions, moving from easier to more difficult.

- *The Big Picture Interactive Bible Storybook: Connecting Christ Throughout God's Story* (The Gospel Project)
- *The Big Picture Story Bible* by David Helm. This book is for young kids. Beautifully illustrated, it walks through the Bible, following the plot line of "God's people in God's place under God's rule." Full confession: I've been known to give this out to parents with preschoolers hoping that the parents would find it as beneficial as the kids.
- *The Jesus Storybook Bible* by Sally Lloyd Jones. This is another book for children. Sally Lloyd Jones does a remarkable job of pointing forward to Jesus, showing how "every story whispers His name." This is the kind of book that demands multiple readings, for adults and children alike.

- *How to Read the Bible through the Jesus Lens: A Guide to Christ-Focused Reading of Scripture* by Michael Williams. This is not a book I would read straight through. Instead, I'd add it to my daily Bible reading. Whenever you read a book of the Bible, you ought to consult Williams's work. He will show you how every book of the Bible ultimately points us to Jesus, and he does so in a way that does justice to each book's particular context and history. Let this book supplement your daily Bible reading.

- *God's Big Picture: Tracing the Storyline of the Bible* by Vaughan Roberts. This book shows how the Bible is telling the story of the kingdom of God. In just a few short chapters, Roberts walks through the story of God's kingdom as it unfolds in the Bible. One of my favorite aspects of this book is the alliteration (the pattern of the kingdom, the perished kingdom, the promised kingdom, the partial kingdom, the prophesied kingdom, the present kingdom, the proclaimed kingdom, and the perfected kingdom). I'm a nerd, I know.

- *The Story of Hope.* This booklet takes the reader through 40 essential Bible scenes (20 Old Testament and 20 New Testament), while distilling eight theological truths from the stories.

- *From Creation to New Creation: Making Sense of the Whole Bible Story* by Tim Chester. Another short book. Chester traces different themes through the Bible, showing how the Scriptures hold together to tell one overarching story.

- *According to Plan: The Unfolding Revelation of God in the Bible* by Graeme Goldsworthy. Graeme Goldsworthy's work shows how the Bible fits together with Christ at the center. Many view this book as a classic, a life-changing resource that helps us see the unveiling of Christ through the pages of Scripture.

- *The True Story of the Whole World: Finding Your Place in the Biblical Drama* by Craig Bartholomew and Michael Goheen. This book is more academic in nature, but it helpfully lays out the story of the Old Testament and shows how everything culminates in the person and work of Jesus Christ.

- *Living God's Word: Discovering Our Place in the Great Story of Scripture* by J. Scott Duvall and J. Daniel Hays. This is a manual for understanding the Bible's story line. A helpful resource that reads like a textbook, you'll want to study this one with a group.

- *The God Who Is There: Finding Your Place in God's Story* by D. A. Carson. As Carson walks through the story line of the Bible, he draws out the theological building blocks essential to Christianity. This book is a more difficult read than some of the others, but one of the most rewarding.

3. Locate Your Teaching in the Grand Narrative.

No matter where you are in Bible study, make sure you orient your people to the Bible Story. Don't leave your people in the weeds of a particular text of Scripture without giving them a compass. Here is an example.

Let's say you are studying a particular topic with your group. The subject for discussion is the "workplace." The main texts for this discussion are from the Proverbs, which do indeed say a lot about work. It's quite possible to mine the proverbs for lessons and principles that will help you in business. But all we will get are helpful suggestions if we fail to connect the proverbs on work to the big story of the Bible.

So, in addition to studying the Proverbs on work, make sure you briefly comment on God's original intention for work (Creation), how work is often toilsome and difficult due to our sin (Fall), how the work of Christ on our behalf transforms our work and makes our labor resound to His glory (Redemption), and how one day our work will be fully satisfying because it will no longer bear the effects of the curse (Restoration). Now you can return to the Proverbs and show how these principles for work make sense within the framework of a biblical worldview. You need to locate your teaching in the grand narrative of Scripture.

Let's say you are studying a particular text of Scripture: the story of Joseph and his brothers. There are a number of ways you could take this text and apply it. I've heard it used as a classic example of forgiveness, as an illustration of good business sense (Joseph set aside grain for the lean years, right?), and as a story of patience and perseverance that good will win out in the end. We can observe these multiple points of application in the passage.

But in addition to these principles, we need to connect the story to the Bible's grand narrative. This story doesn't happen in a vacuum. God has decided to bless the children of Abraham, and He has promised to bless the whole world through Abraham's descendants. We see a foreshadowing of that future blessing right here, don't we? Joseph is betrayed by his brothers and suffers unjustly at the hands of the rulers. But through these acts of injustice, God providentially lifts Joseph to the position from which his influence will lead the world to be saved from a terrible famine. The evil actions committed against Joseph God turned to good.

So, the story of Joseph—while certainly an example of forgiveness, foresight, and good triumphing over evil—points forward to an even greater rescue, when Jesus will be betrayed by his brothers, will suffer unjustly at the hands of the rulers, before being raised from the dead to bring the blessing of salvation to all the people of the world. The evil actions committed against Jesus on the cross become the catalyst for redemption. Pastor W. A. Criswell, when preaching on Joseph went so far as to say this is a story of Christ and Calvary in miniature.[6]

No matter where you are in the biblical story line, spend a few minutes pointing backward and forward. Help people get oriented to the Bible as a whole. Don't shy away from offering some clear, useful principles for interpreting the Bible. Ultimately, you want people to get the lay of the land and be equipped to study the Bible on their own.

4. Point to Jesus as the Ultimate Answer to Our Sin Problem.

Whenever you point forward in the Bible, you want to make sure you point to Jesus in a way that is clear and compelling. We're not seeking imaginative readings of the Bible. It's not only important that we point people to Jesus. It also matters how we point to Jesus.

When we were talking through the core values of The Gospel Project, I recall a conversation about Christ-centeredness and the right and wrong way to point people to Jesus. One pastor told us, "Be careful that when you point people to Jesus, you're not simply demonstrating the cleverness of your own interpretation." He was cautioning us against trying to find Christ under every rock and behind every bush in the Old Testament.

The danger of over-reading the Bible is that the people you lead will eventually become more dependent on you as the teacher and less dependent on the Word itself. They'll be more amazed at your skill of finding Jesus everywhere than they will be astonished to encounter Jesus as the Bible reveals Him.

There is ongoing debate about the right and wrong ways to point ahead to Jesus, but everyone agrees that the Old Testament anticipates the coming of Christ. After all, on the road to Emmaus, Jesus told His disciples how the Old Testament was about Him. Still, we can't allegorize Bible stories and make them something they're not. It's not appropriate to say that the "scarlet cord" hanging from Rahab's window in Jericho represents the blood of Jesus that saves us from destruction. What is appropriate is to say this: "Rahab demonstrated her faith in the one true God by obeying the instructions of God's people. God saw her faith and kept His promise to Rahab and her family. In fact, God placed Rahab in the family line of Jesus Himself, the Savior whose life represents the ultimate example of God keeping His promises and delivering people who trust in Him."

5. Challenge people, but stay accessible.

It's best to expect a lot out of those who attend a small group or Sunday school class. Set the bar high, and watch people rise to the occasion. There's no need to adopt a "No Child Left Behind" mentality, as if we can and should go only as deep as the least knowledgeable person in the group. We don't think this way in real life. When our son was still on baby food, we didn't stop eating steak and potatoes. Neither did we stop feeding our son solid food when our daughter came along. Instead, we gathered as a family and ate together.

As a group leader, you want to provide a feast and let people draw the sustenance they need. But we may have to "cut up the meat" for new believers and make sure that the truth is accessible. The key is to put the biblical ingredients together and provide the meal. Fill up the plate! Don't be afraid to challenge people, just make sure you are continually thinking of ways to drive the point home.

Take the Long View

I still remember the kids' team meeting for The Gospel Project where we looked through the list of Bible stories we were going to introduce to children. Session 5 was the story of Job, not a story you come across very often in children's literature.

The decision to tell kids—even preschoolers—the story of Job wasn't hard to make. We'd already decided that we wanted to challenge kids with The Gospel Project material. If we were doing a lesson on Obadiah, why not Job?

But how would we make the Christ connection? Would we really introduce a big word like "mediator" to three- and four-year-olds? Here's what we wanted to tell kids: Job's suffering and his request for a mediator give us a glimpse of our Savior, Jesus. Neither Job nor Jesus experienced suffering because they sinned. Unlike Job, Jesus never questioned why He had to suffer. Jesus understood that we needed Him to pay the price for our sin and be our mediator before God.

I remember thinking about my daughter, Julia, as we had this conversation. She was three at the time. My wife and I were frequent fill-in teachers for Julia's preschool group in our church. I saw those cute, rambunctious kids in my mind as we discussed how to present the story of Job and the Christ connection.

The question came up, "Will a preschooler have a clue what we're talking about? How much of the story will they get?" After some good discussion, we decided they probably wouldn't understand it all.

So did we ditch the idea? No. Instead, we decided to introduce the word "mediator" to preschoolers. We would simplify the Christ connections for preschoolers, and we'd make sure we explain what big words mean, but we would not shy away from a four-syllable word that helped point them to Christ.

In the end, we made a decision to take the long view with regard to Bible teaching instead of just thinking about individual lessons. That's what all teachers need to do, regardless of age group. You need to recognize that some of your words or phrases or theological concepts might go over their heads. Your group might not remember all the information you give them. But if you connect that information to the grand narrative of Scripture, and continually point them to Jesus, they'll get what's most important.

I don't expect my daughter to come home explaining to me in great detail what a mediator is. But I'm glad to know that the next time she hears this story, she'll already have an important word in the back of her mind. And I'm glad to know that whatever the story, she has teachers pointing her to Jesus. The point isn't filling little heads with theological knowledge but introducing little hearts to the big God who has revealed Himself to us in Jesus Christ.

Every night, I pray the Lord's Prayer with my kids. Right now, my daughter knows the words by heart. And yes, I know she is praying big words like "hallowed," "kingdom," "debts," and "temptation," words she doesn't quite understand. What to do? Should I steer clear from the Lord's Prayer? Not at all.

I'm praying my daughter grows up into those words. I look at her the same way I look at a kid trying on Mama's shoes. The feet are too small and the shoes are too big, but one of these days, she'll grow up and they'll fit. That's how we pray. That's why we introduce the big truths of the Bible. That's why we teach our kids the Bible stories that challenge their assumptions, raise expectations, and point them to Jesus.

Small kids need big words. Not because they understand everything all at once but because, over time, God uses the inspired words of His Book to convict kids of sin and convince them to repent and believe in Christ.

"Repent and believe." Those are big words too. That's why even now I'm praying for the day those two big words represent the reality of my kids' little hearts. Showing how all the Bible points to Jesus is one way of making sure they see the Savior.

Like the children in your kids' small groups, adults in your groups need gospel-centered teaching made accessible for them too. After all, the apostle Paul referred to his disciples as his "beloved" and "little ones." But like our children, don't be afraid to wade in the deep waters of the gospel alongside new believers. It won't be long before they will need to know how to teach others to swim.

4

Ground Your Application in the Gospel

 We've looked at the first question you should ask of every lesson you prepare, a question that takes you back to the grand narrative of Scripture and gives you a worldview-tinged aspect to your Bible study. Now, we arrive at the next question, one that is even more important: "What is distinctively Christian about the way I am addressing this topic or passage?"

This kind of question sounds simple, and it is . . . on the surface. But beneath this question is something more profound, a way to make sure the content you provide connects back the gospel. We're going to further explore application by offering three additional questions that make sure we are driving back to the gospel when we teach the Bible.

What Is Christian?

Simply saying, "What's Christian about my lesson?" won't be enough for gospel-centered application, unless we once again connect gospel and Christianity the way it should be. The word "Christian" has a whole set of meanings and connotations in evangelical circles today.

When I was a teenager, there was a debate in our student ministry about what constituted "Christian music." During the heyday of "CCM," there were artists who were crossing over to secular radio and back again to Christian radio, blurring the lines of what made music "Christian." Is this song Christian because of the lyrics? Do the lyrics specifically say something about Jesus? Or something spiritual? Is this song Christian because it was written by a Christian and displays the worldview of someone who follows Christ, even if there is nothing in it that mentions

God or Jesus? Is this song Christian because it's performed by a Christian band?

Those conversations about what made something "Christian" left me wondering if it's appropriate to use the word "Christian" as an adjective rather than a noun. Based on the choices of Christian radio show hosts, I suspect that nowadays "Christian" is synonymous with music that was "safe for the whole family," or it refers to music from a singer whose lyrics have a vaguely Christian, spiritual element to it. Almost anything "spiritual" could make the cut. As long as there was some mention of God or "heaven," the song was considered "Christian."

Without digressing into a conversation about art and if it can or should be considered "Christian" (a conversation worth having, but not within the constraints of this kind of book), the "what makes music Christian?" question brings up a foundational issue for how we approach Bible study. Is your lesson or Bible study "Christian" simply because it mentions Jesus? Because it has the Bible as its base? Because it leads to spiritual application?

I don't think so. In fact, I think a lot of what passes for Bible study these days isn't necessarily Christian at all. Don't misunderstand me; I'm not saying that Christians are not involved in leading these studies, or that the people participating in these small groups are not Christian. I'm speaking specifically of the content of our message. Is it Christian? The question is not, "*Do* you open the Bible and comment on it?" but "*How* do you open the Bible and comment on it?"

At the end of the day, unless we bring people back to the gospel, we are not offering anything distinctively Christian in our small groups. We may be commenting on Christian Scripture, pulling out good points of application, and offering solid information. But it's the gospel that makes our teaching distinctively Christian. It's the gospel that separates our study from mere moralistic suggestions or information overload.

When understood rightly, "What is *distinctively* Christian about how I am approaching this topic or passage?" will lead you back to the gospel because it focuses on that key word *distinctively*. The distinctively Christian thing about Christianity is Christ and His grace. It's the good news about how He died on the cross for our sins and rose from the grave on the third day.

So how do we ensure that our preaching and teaching gets to Jesus? I suggest three follow-up questions that help us analyze our content in light of the gospel.

1. Is there anything about my treatment of this Old Testament text that a faithful Jew could not affirm?

Why is this a helpful question? Because it reminds us to approach the Old Testament from the perspective of a Christian who believes the whole Bible points to Jesus Christ. We spent some time on this point in the previous chapter, so I won't belabor it again. But it deserves repeating: Failure to point to Jesus in your lesson means that your message is not distinctively Christian.

If you preach the story of Moses and the Passover and do not point forward to our Passover Lamb who takes away the sins of the world, then you are teaching from Exodus much like a rabbi, not like a Christian herald of the gospel. If you preach individual proverbs and bring all sorts of application out of the wisdom literature without ever showing how Christ is our Wisdom (2 Cor. 1), then you haven't delivered a distinctively Christian message. If you preach the narratives of the kings in the Old Testament and only draw out moral lessons from their examples, then you have forgotten how the kings (both good ones and bad ones) are intended to evoke a sense of longing and anticipation for the King of kings who will usher in His kingdom through the sacrificial ministry of His death and the smashing victory of His resurrection.

On the road to Emmaus, Jesus told His disciples that the Old Testament pointed to Him. Disciples who take Jesus' words seriously will approach Old Testament texts, not only to mine them for practical ways to live, but also to see how they point us to the Savior. I love how the confessional statement of my denomination puts it: "All Scripture is a testimony to Christ, who is Himself the focus of divine revelation." Did you catch that first word? All Scripture is a testimony to Christ, even the Scriptures that don't explicitly mention Him.

So, when you preach from the Old Testament, it's imperative that you point people forward to the Messiah. It's what makes your message distinctively Christian.

2. Is there anything about my treatment of this New Testament text that a Mormon could not affirm?

This question isn't meant to single out Mormons, but to make sure we understand that you can talk a lot about Jesus and still not have a distinctively Christian message. After all, Mormons talk about Jesus. Jehovah's Witnesses talk about Jesus. Muslims talk about Isa. And on television, there are plenty of preachers who talk about Jesus, whose message couldn't be designated truly "Christian" in any recognizable way.

You may be thinking, "Wait a minute! You're telling me that a message can have Jesus in it and still not be Christian?" Absolutely. The Gnostic Gospels, written long after the Gospels we have in our Bibles, are filled with teachings about Jesus and teachings from Jesus (supposedly). Unfortunately, these teachings aren't true. The Jesus described in the Bible is missing, and instead, we get a pious, mysterious sage who spouts "other-worldly wisdom" and "secret knowledge." The true Jesus is missing.

What makes a message distinctively Christian is not that someone named Jesus is mentioned throughout. It's not that we mention Jesus, but what we say about Jesus that matters. We must be sure we are presenting the biblical Jesus, and not a Jesus of our own imagination.

Let me bring this a little closer to home, since I'm pretty sure that few of us are presenting a "Mormon Jesus" in our lessons. Let's say you are teaching a Gospel narrative about how Jesus healed blind Bartimaeus. Now, you can find all sorts of moral truths about Bartimaeus: he was persistent, he addressed Jesus correctly, he ignored those who would hold him back, etc. But do these points of application mean you have presented a distinctively Christian message? No. Not unless you point forward to the truth of Jesus Christ crucified and raised, Savior and Lord of the world.

You see, other religions will present Jesus as a miracle-worker. Self-help preachers will mine these stories for application points that sell lots of books. But unless Jesus is presented as the Son of God, the sinless Savior who died and rose again, we have not presented a message about Jesus that is distinctively Christian. We haven't gotten back to the gospel.

Ed Stetzer often says that he never wants to preach a sermon that could be true had Jesus not died and been raised. I love that. It immediately gives clarity to the way we talk about Jesus. It not only ensures that Christ is present in the lesson, but that He is present as Savior and Lord. It turns the focus away from ourselves and makes Christ the Hero. It keeps us from presenting Jesus as if He were merely a life coach, someone to help us along in the life we've chosen for ourselves. Instead, it puts forth a sovereign King who, out of love for us, requires our obedience and then gives His life to purchase our salvation. We must make sure we do not present Jesus only as a moral example, but that we present Him as the only Savior, the One who calls for repentance and faith.

3. Is there anything in my application that an unbeliever off the street would be uncomfortable with?

At first glance, this question appears to be one of those "seeker-sensitive" concerns, doesn't it? You may be thinking, "Does this mean we should make sure people don't find our teaching uncomfortable?" Actually, I'm saying the opposite. You should make sure that your application is connected to the gospel in a way where the unbelieving person senses a difference between "morality" and "the gospel." You want your application to go beyond "be a nice person."

Example 1: Marital Love

Let's say you are leading a group around Father's Day, and the application for your lesson is: "Husbands ought to love their wives." That's certainly not a bad application, is it? It's biblical. It's concise.

Now, let's ask the question, "Is there anything in this application that an unbeliever would have a problem with?" Probably not. I bet if we surveyed most people in North America and asked them if they agreed with the statement, "Husbands ought to love their wives," most would say, "Yes."

If this application is as far as you go as a leader, then the husbands in your group will interpret that statement in their own way. One guy will be thinking, "I guess I ought to compliment my wife more often." The next guy will think, "Maybe I should help around the house more." The natural response is for a husband to have his own conception of what loving his wife looks like. There's nothing particularly biblical about his vision. He's filling that application with his own perspective.

So how do we tighten up this application to focus on Jesus? How do we make sure we're not just offering a biblical, moral message that even an unbeliever would affirm? How do we take it back to the gospel? By doing what Paul did.

The apostle Paul wrote: "Husbands love your wives as Christ loved the church and gave Himself for her" (Eph. 5:25). Whoa! That's where the unbeliever sees something that goes beyond mere morality. Now, we're talking about what Jesus has done for us and how Jesus' work shapes what a husband's love looks like. Now, you've got men in your group who start realizing that their love for their wives must be formed by the cross. It's self-sacrificial. It's self-giving. It's more than getting your hands wet in the kitchen sink. A husband who loves his wife in this way must be willing to die for her.

Do you see what we've done? We've connected the application point back to the gospel, showing the unbeliever what a distinctively Christian view of marital love looks like and showing the believer how his love must flow from Christ's love from us. It's not just a moral command. It's a moral command that is grounded in the gospel of Jesus Christ.

Example 2: Generosity

Let's say you're teaching on stewardship, and your application point is "We ought to be generous with our money" or "We ought to give our resources to help those in need." Those are both true, biblical statements. Now, let's ask the question of those application points. Would an unbeliever off the street have a problem with those statements? Probably not. In fact, most decent, upstanding citizens in our society would agree that people ought to be generous. Even people from other religions say the same thing. After all, almsgiving is one of the five pillars of Islam!

So, even if the application is good, there is no gospel. It is a moral application that most anyone would agree with. Furthermore, the people in your group will begin to interpret "generosity" through the lens of their own definition. They'll start thinking, "I guess I ought to give more to the church. Maybe I should start tithing." Or they'll feel guilty for what they have in comparison to those in need, and they'll sponsor a child in Africa. Some in your group, if they take the application to heart, will make little adjustments here and there.

So, what should we do? Again, we look to the apostle Paul who, when he spoke about generosity, grounded his command in the gospel of Christ giving His all for our salvation. We say, "We ought to be generous with our money, just as Christ, 'though He was rich, for your sake He became poor" (2 Cor. 8:9). Suddenly, we realize that our view of "generosity" shouldn't be formed by how the world defines the word. Instead, we see Christ giving everything—pouring Himself out for the sake of God's mission. Now, generosity begins to look radical. As we are confronted again and again with the glorious gospel of Christ giving up everything to purchase our salvation, we begin to have a stronger understanding of what gospel-shaped generosity looks like. It's not motivated by guilt, but by grace.

I remember sitting in a small group once, and we were discussing the story of how Zacchaeus, the "wee little man" who hosted Jesus in his home, repented of his greed and volunteered to pay people back four times the amount he had cheated them. As our group was discussing the passage, we talked about tithing and giving above and beyond what's expected. One of the guys in our group said, "I just wish it had been spelled out for us exactly what we should be giving above ten percent. Then, we'd know we'd fulfilled the requirement." My response went like this: "If God had given us a 'requirement,' we would miss the point. The point wasn't that Zacchaeus gave exactly what Jesus asked for. Jesus didn't even tell him what to do. The point was that Zacchaeus encountered Christ, and he couldn't help but be generous. We don't need an Excel spreadsheet to tell us how much to give and when we've satisfied the requirement. We need an encounter with Christ so that we give passionately, joyfully, and extravagantly. That's how we find satisfaction in giving."

Example 3: Forgiveness

Watch television shows like Dr. Phil, and you often hear hosts challenge victims to forgive anyone who has wronged them. Most of the time, forgiveness is viewed in therapeutic terms that will help the victim. "Forgiving" is about "letting go," refusing to drag around that weight of offense against another person. The reason you should forgive is for your own benefit.

Contrast this view of forgiveness with the Christian understanding, that we are to be kind and tenderhearted, "forgiving one another just as God also forgave you in Christ" (Eph. 4:32). Our forgiveness of others flows from God's forgiveness of us. God didn't forgive us because He needed to; He forgave because of His love for us. Likewise, we don't forgive others because it's good for us, but because we know how much we have been forgiven. The more we recognize the state of our own sinfulness, the more we are blown away by the truth that God loved us anyway, so much so that He sent His Son to die for us.

Example 4: Temptation

It's possible to use a story with Jesus in a way that fails to focus on the gospel. Sometimes this happens with the temptation scene of Jesus in the New Testament. The application will be something like this: We all go through temptation, but if we follow the strategy of Jesus, we can resist temptation. So let's read our Bibles and commit Scripture to memory like Jesus did!

There's certainly nothing unbiblical about applying the temptation scene in this way, but if this is all we say, we give the impression that we overcome temptation by scrunching up our willpower and resisting by sheer force. The point of the temptation scene, however, is to show how Jesus overcame temptation in our place. Where Adam failed in the garden, and Israel failed in the wilderness, Jesus succeeded. He obeys in our place.

The way to apply the temptation scene, then, is not merely to mention Jesus' strategies for resisting Satan, but also to show that it's only because Christ overcame temptation that we have any hope at all. We resist Satan not through willpower, but through the Spirit's power given freely to us because of Christ's perfect obedience in the wilderness and His sacrificial death on Calvary.

Back to the Gospel

We could go on and on. When we tell people not to lie, we should connect that application back to Jesus, who is the Truth. When we tell men and women to not commit adultery, we show how marital infidelity rips apart a picture of God's faithful love shown to us in the gospel. When we talk about church attendance, we don't just stress the way it benefits us, as if it were a sports club or a country club; instead, we go back to the reality that the church has been constituted as a people, bought by the blood of Christ. When we encourage hospitality, we do so as people who were once strangers welcomed into the family of God. When we go over the Ten Commandments, we let Jesus' intensification of the Commandments drive us to our knees in repentance, so that we can then look up and see how Jesus fulfills the Commandments in our place and now gives us His Spirit, who empowers our obedience.

If we are to be Christian leaders delivering Christian content, then we must be centered on the message that only Christianity has to offer—the gospel. Our application should not start with "Who am I and what should I do?" but "Who is Christ and what has He done?" Answer those questions first. Concentrate on who you are in Christ before moving on to what you should do as a Christian.

Too many times, leaders and teachers think that the way to get a person motivated to obedience is to give them a lot of do's and don'ts, a list of practical ways to apply the truth of the Scriptures. But focusing too heavily on application makes it seem like the Bible is all about us. Instead, we ought to consider the words of G. K. Chesterton, who was surely right to say, "How much larger your life would be if your self could become smaller in it!" If we were to connect that line to Bible study, we could put it this way: "How much larger your Bible study would be if your self could become smaller in it!"[7] Go to the Bible looking for God. Find Him, and application will follow. But go looking for application, and you may miss both.

More than a hundred years ago, Oswald Chambers wrote about the gospel being the most important aspect of the Christian's life. "Our calling is not primarily to be holy men and women, but to be proclaimers of the gospel of God. The one all-important thing is that the gospel of God should be recognized as the abiding reality." He reminded his readers that "personal holiness is an effect of redemption, not the cause of it," implying that Christ's redemption ought to be the center of the Christian life—not our journey of increasing holiness. In fact, Chambers recognized the counterproductive nature of focusing too much on application rather than the gospel. "Paul was not overly interested in his own character. And as long as our eyes are focused on our own personal holiness, we will never even get close to the full reality of redemption. Christian workers fail because they place their desire for their own holiness above their desire to know God. . . . God cannot deliver me while my interest is merely in my own character. Paul was not conscious of himself. He was recklessly abandoned, totally surrendered, and separated by God for one purpose—to proclaim the gospel of God."[8]

Application with merely the occasional mention of redemption is like trying to turn on the lights when the plug is loosely dangling from the outlet. Focus on redemption in a way that shows how application flows from Christ's work, and you've secured the power source. When you flip the switch, light floods the dark room.

Remember where the power of God is—the gospel.

5

Overflow with Passion
for God's Mission

 We've looked at two questions we should ask of the content in our teaching:

1.   How does this passage or topic fit into the grand narrative of Scripture?

2.   What is distinctively Christian about the way I am addressing this topic or passage?

A third question is vitally important if we hope to connect the gospel to our mission as Christ's followers: "How does this truth equip God's church to live on mission?"

Evangelical Christians sometimes talk about what the Bible *is* more than what the Bible *does*. In other words, our focus is on the inspired nature of the biblical text, not so much on what the inspired biblical text is intended to do.

Don't misunderstand—never for a moment should we waver on the truth of God's inspired Word. If the Bible is merely a record of God's interactions with people in the past and not the inspired, inerrant Word of God to us today, then we have no ultimate authority to submit to. We are left with our own whims and preferences instead of the unchanging, authoritative Word of God.

But let's be clear. It's not enough to participate in Bible study as if the purpose of our study is merely to know and love these inspired words. No. The purpose for which God gave us His Word is that we might be fully equipped to do His will. In a very real sense, we have not truly understood God's Word unless we have begun to obey it. Head knowledge of the truth is not enough. Heart knowledge of the Truth-giver is not enough. At some point, the head and the heart must move the hands into service and the feet into mission.

Therefore, a gospel-centered teacher will seek to show how the truths of the Bible equip God's church to live on mission. Doctrine does not exist for its own sake. We study the truths of God's Word, so that our hearts may be engaged with our Maker, and our hands and feet be moved to action.

Teaching cannot properly be considered "gospel-centered" unless it has a missionary shape to it. Unless the truths of God's Word are leading us to mission, we are just studying the gospel as a closed group of like-minded Christians, not an all-embracing group of fervent ambassadors for King Jesus. Miss the mission, and you've missed the point of gospel-centrality.

Mission Mirrors God

There is no true gospel-centeredness that does not lead to mission, because the gospel is the story of a God with a missionary heart, a Father who desires that all come to repentance, a Shepherd who seeks and saves the one lost sheep. The purpose of God's Word is to reveal God and His plan to us, in order that we might then be empowered to fulfill His Great Commission. God's plan is that people from every tongue, tribe, and nation would bring Him glory. When we study the Bible, we ought to see it in light of its purpose—to equip us to be God's missionaries in our communities and around the world.

The more we grow in our faith and become like Jesus, the more the heart of Jesus should be evident in our own lives. What greater evidence is there of a Christlike heart than passion for God's mission? What greater evidence is there that the truth of the gospel has soaked into someone's life than seeing passion for the lost overflow through our witness? The gospel-centered believer will take on the role of a servant, just as Jesus served us through His life, death, and resurrection. We serve our neighbors out of love, doing good to those around us, showing the love of Christ, and sharing the good news of salvation.

Mission mirrors God. We show others who God is and what He is like by the way we live. It's not enough to talk about the gospel in our groups. We need to recognize that the Bible intends to reorient our lives around God's mission and equip us to join Him in the work He is doing.

Ask the "How does this lead to mission?" question in order to give your lessons a missional orientation.

Mission Motivated by the Gospel

A second reason the "mission" question is necessary is because it reminds us of the integral connection between the gospel and mission. When properly understood, the gospel is the basis for mission. We celebrate the gospel as people consumed by the gospel. The goal is that our celebration of the gospel will result in greater and wider circles of people who hear the good news and join the mission.

A pastor recently asked me about the missional strategy behind The Gospel Project curriculum. "We've got people in small groups who study the Scriptures but aren't involved in reaching out to their community with the gospel," he said. "How can I get them motivated?"

In response, I mentioned how our natural tendency as church leaders is to reinforce the commands related to our mission, to tell people again and again what they should be doing. We think, *If they aren't reaching out to represent and proclaim Christ, they must not know what to do.*

But is this really the case? In my experience, the problem isn't that we've forgotten our responsibility to love our neighbor and share the gospel. The problem is that even when we know what our duty is, we still don't do it. The problem is deeper. It's a want-to problem, not an I-don't-know problem.

That's why I'm convinced that focusing most of your teaching on our missional duty isn't the best way to motivate people to serve Christ long-term. It may result in some initial fruit, but it doesn't effect the heart-change necessary for long-lasting obedience. An army of begrudging, guilt-ridden evangelists "doing their duty" is not likely to attract many converts. The goal is to see a delight-filled group of Christians overflowing with love for God and neighbor who can't help but speak of the One who loved them and gave Himself for them.

So what to do? It's pretty simple, actually. Exalt God. Magnify His holiness. Praise His greatness. Exult in His grace. Don't spend all your time thinking of creative ways to get across the command of evangelism and missions (though there is a time and place for such thinking). Instead, spend your time exalting the God of mission, trusting that an awe-inspiring vision of His majesty will set your people's feet on the right course.

Set the magnificent, majestic God of the Bible before your people week after week, and pray that they will encounter Him for who He is. Why? Because it's an encounter with an awesome God that motivates us to mission.

Mission Encounters

Case in point: our biblical heroes. As you read through the Bible, you'll notice that whenever people come face to face with God's greatness, the next scene often shows them on mission.

Moses trembled before God in the burning bush. Next he was standing before Pharaoh saying, "Let my people go!" The majesty of God displayed before Moses' eyes on a faraway hillside is the same majesty God displays before the greatest empire of the day.

Isaiah caught a vision of the Lord in His temple that was so staggering that he fell on his face like a dead man. Notice God didn't even have to tell him what to do. God simply asked, "Who will go for us?" The awestruck Isaiah volunteered: "Here am I. Send me." (Isa. 6:8).

The Samaritan woman at the well was amazed at the supernatural knowledge of Jesus. Next we see her running into town telling her friends and family about His greatness.

The women at the tomb were the first to witness the resurrection power of God. Next we see them telling everyone, "We have seen the Lord!"

Peter denied Christ and hid in a locked room. After encountering the greatness of King Jesus, we see him boldly proclaiming Christ as Messiah and Lord before thousands of people.

Paul went from being a terrorist persecutor of Christians to the greatest missionary the world has ever known. What happened? He had an encounter with the risen Jesus, and he spent the rest of his life seeking to help the Gentiles see the very One who initially blinded him.

Why should it be any different with us? Missional fruitfulness comes from a heart gripped by God's greatness and enthralled with His grace. We ought to be so mesmerized by the glory of Jesus Christ that we count it as nothing to lose our lives for the spread of His fame. Our goal is to lead our groups to get on our faces before God and then get on our feet for His mission.

Mission Birthed by Worship

Lack of mission is rarely a knowledge problem; it's a worship problem. We don't have any trouble talking about the things we love most. Whenever we find something worthy of attention, we talk about it. The same is true of our relationship with Christ. The more we are in awe of His worthiness, the more likely we are to speak of Him to others.

Sometimes, people worry that the rough edges of Christianity will lead us to avoid serving our neighbor and sharing the gospel. So we play down some of the harder truths of the gospel, not denying them of course, but not giving them their proper weight.

The reality of hell is an example. There are all sorts of ways to downplay the truth of one's eternal destiny; the most common is simply to not speak of it, or to recast salvation as dealing more with this life than the next.

But what happens when the reality of hell is no longer grounding our talk about salvation and the gospel? We miss out on a moment of worship. Consider this scenario. You're walking with a friend, not paying much attention to where you are headed. Suddenly, your friend grabs your arm and yanks you backward. At first, you are annoyed that you've been stopped so suddenly. But then your friend points in front of you. Sure enough, he had a reason. You were about to step off into a ditch, where you might have broken your foot or sprained your ankle. Your annoyance turns to gratitude for his "saving you" from possible harm. You thank your friend and move on.

Consider the same scenario, except this time your friend doesn't pull you back from a ditch, but a cliff. You were about to fall to your death, hundreds of feet below.

What would your reaction be in this situation? Not just a word of "thanks." You'd be crying and hugging your friend, overflowing with gratitude for the way he just saved your life.

In the same way, when we minimize the severity of God's judgment for sin, we are less inclined to stand in awe of the marvelous salvation Christ has provided for us. We think we're pushing aside an obstacle when we neglect the reality of judgment. But what we're actually doing is pushing away one of the truths that most leads us to worship. The reality of God's grace is all the more amazing the more we see our sin and what it deserves.

A gospel-centered teacher isn't satisfied to see the group learn truths about God. A gospel-centered truth wants the group to feel those truths. To feel the full weight of God's provision for us in Christ. To have the heart's affections stirred to worship of the loving God who has saved us by His grace and incorporated us into His family.

What's at stake when we rush toward application? We can sometimes short-circuit the moment of awe that the

Scriptures intend to evoke. We hurry to the practical so fast we miss the powerful!

Not long ago, I was speaking to a group of student ministers on this very subject. We were talking about our tendency to become so familiar with some of the stories in the Bible that we are no longer awed by the truth of the narrative. I used the story of Jesus calming the storm as an example. How many of us hurry so quickly to apply that story to "Jesus' presence with us during the storms of life" that we miss the moment of awe that led the disciples to say, "What kind of man is this?—even the winds and seas obey Him!" (Matt. 8:27). It's fine to apply the account of Jesus calming the storm in various ways. But don't rush to that application so quickly you miss the moment of awe.

A few days after my talk with the student ministers, one of them sent me a tweet, saying, "I couldn't sleep last night thinking . . . He really did silence the storm. Crazy." The student minister had gone from over-familiarization with a famous story of Scripture to once again being captured by the power of the narrative. He marveled at the power of Jesus, which is exactly what the biblical authors intended our reaction to be.

Rushing to application is a sign that we are bored with the Bible. Fight the temptation. Make sure you get to mission, but first, give people the unvarnished Jesus.

Overflow with Passion

I want to end this little book with a special word to teachers and group leaders. Whatever literature you may use, you are the factor that makes the difference. Gospel-fueled transformation takes place best when the teacher's life is bubbling over with gospel enthusiasm.

So let's ask ourselves:

- Am I reading my Bible just to prepare my lesson? Or am I immersed in this gospel story daily?
- Am I reading other literature and materials that deepen my own walk with Christ? Or am I content with throwing together the facts for an interesting presentation on Sunday morning?

- Am I seeking to be a missionary in the community God has placed me? Or am I content with the little group I teach on the weekend?

Deeper teaching happens when we have deeper teachers. Your group won't remember everything you teach them, but they will probably remember what you're most excited about.

Teachers and group leaders, it's important that we believe the gospel; it's also important that we celebrate this gospel in a way that makes clear it is "of first importance."

What your group celebrates corporately is just as important as what your group affirms doctrinally. Celebrate the gospel, and cross-cultural ministry will bubble up in surprising ways. Celebrate your church's personal preferences, and your group will become an insular group of like-minded individuals. Celebrate your own gifts as leader, and your group will be centered on you as the hero rather than Jesus.

Conclusion

If there's one thing we need to be clear about in our preaching and teaching, it's the gospel announcement that Jesus Christ, the Son of God, lived a perfect life in our place, died on the cross for the sins of the world, rose again to launch God's new creation, and is now exalted as Lord of the world. In response to this message, we must call people to repent and believe. And as Christians, we must continue living every day in repentant faith, witnessing to the love of our great God.

So fellow teachers, let's soak ourselves in the truths of the gospel and the Word. Then, let's invite others to the fountain of living water offered freely by our Master Teacher whose life and death changes everything.

Notes

1. Herschel H. Hobbs, *The Baptist Faith and Message*, Rev. Ed. (Nashville: LifeWay Church Resources, 2002), 22–24, 35.

2. "When I Survey the Wondrous Cross" by Isaac Watts, 1707.

3. The Gospel Project is a Bible study curriculum I helped develop at LifeWay Christian Resources. The curriculum is offered for children, students, and adults.

4. Moralistic therapeutic deism is explained in detail in *Soul Searching: The Religious and Spiritual Lives of American Teenagers* by Christian Smith and Melina Lundquist Denton, Oxford University Press, reprint, 2009.

5. "In short, the good news of Jesus Christ is virtually incoherent unless it is securely set into a biblical worldview." D. A. Carson, *The Gagging of God* (Grand Rapids: Zondervan, 1996), 502.

6. W. A. Criswell's sermon can be found at http://dev.wac-riswell.com/sermons/1989/the-coat-of-many-colors.

7. G. K. Chesterton, *Orthodoxy* (London: John Lane, 1909), 34–35.

8. Oswald Chambers, *My Utmost for His Highest*, Updated Edition (Grand Rapids: Discovery House Publishers, 1992), 31.